大切ないつもの暮らし

大切ないつもの暮らし

2011年3月11日、あの地震は起こりました。私は職場（東京都中野区）のギャラリーの受付に座っていました。窓からは午後の穏やかな日の光が差し込み、数名のお客様が来廊されていて、それまでは平穏な時間が流れていました。午後2時46分、ぐらぐらと地震が起こり、最初は、たまにあるような軽い地震かと思っていましたが、揺れが強くなり、しかも長い時間揺れて、書籍スペースに置かれた本の一部が飛び出して床に散乱し、私は外に逃げるべきかどうか考えながらも、何もできず立ち尽くしている間に、最初の強く長い地震は収まりました。その後も余震が続き、電車は止まり、私は帰宅困難となり、翌日やっとの思いで自宅（神奈川県川崎市）に辿り着きました。ニュースで被災地の惨状を知りあまりの酷さに驚愕し、福島第一原子力発電所の事故に言葉を無くしました。スーパーからは食料品や水が無くなり、電力不足による計画停電が始まりました。ついさっきまで平穏に暮らしていたのに、一瞬にして、本当に一瞬にして、多くの人が普通の暮しを無くしてしまいました。いとも簡単に。被災地の方々の状況は、これとは比べ物にならない、言葉では言い尽くせないほど過酷なものだと思います。この東日本大震災をきっかけに、普通に過ごせることの大切さを一段と強く感じるようになりました。

そもそも、普通の暮しを大切に思うようになったのは、夭折した私の親戚達の影響があると思います。私の父方の伯父と母方の伯父は太平洋戦争へ出征し、二人とも生きて戻ってくることはありませんでした。私の伯母と3人の幼いいとこは、昭和32年長崎県諫早市で起こった諫早大水害で、氾濫した河に家ごと流されて亡くなりました。父は運良く外出していて生き残りましたが、家も家族も亡くしてしまいました。母は満州の引き上げで、出征した伯父以外の家族は生きて帰国できましたが全財産を無くしました。やがて父と母は結婚し、兄と私が生まれました。

災害に見舞われて亡くなったり、家や家族を失ったりする人たちは、自分とは遠い特別不運な誰かではなくて、誰にでも起こりうることなのだと痛感します。そして不幸はある日突然やってくるのだと。災害以外でも、ある人は病気で、ある人は事故で、ある人は家族や友人の死で、ある人は失業で、ある人は人間関係で、ある日突然、平穏な暮しが無くなってしまうと。だからこそ、普通に過ごせることを大切にしなければいけないと強く感じます。私の伯父、伯母、いとこ達は私の生前に亡くなったので会ったことも無いけれど、いつも私の頭の片隅にそのことがあって、私の生き方に影響を与えていると思います。伯父、伯母等の死が、普通の暮しの大切さを教えてくれて、私にその事を残していってくれたと思っています。

2012年3月　田中由美子

The Precious Daily Life in Japan

On March 11, 2011, the earthquake occurred. I was sitting at the reception desk in the gallery where I work – Nakano – ward, Tokyo. The mild afternoon sunlight was shining in through the window. Several visitors were looking around the gallery. It had been peaceful and quiet. At 2:46 p.m. there came a sudden violent quake. I thought it was one of the minor earthquakes that we occasionally have. But the quakes were getting bigger. Books began to jump out of the shelves and get scattered around the floor. Though I thought of running out of the building for safety's sake, I could do nothing but stand helplessly where I was until these long violent shocks subsided. Subsequently the aftershocks continued, and the train services were badly interrupted. It was the next day that I finally came back home in Kawasaki-city, Kanagawa Prefecture. I learned about the disaster-stricken area on the news. I was shocked by the unprecedented extent of the damage. The horror of the Fukushima Daiichi nuclear disaster left me speechless. Soon food and water were gone from the stores. The electric power company launched the planned blackouts due to the power shortage. A while ago, people did live a peaceful life. But now it was gone. Many of us were deprived of our ordinary life all too soon. But the condition of the disaster area was far worse, and its severity no words could describe. How precious it is to be able to live an ordinary life, this Great East Japan Earthquake led me to realize more keenly than before.

My particular feeling toward the ordinary life above has its roots in the circumstances which led to some of my relatives' young death long ago. Both my paternal and maternal uncles went to the front in the Pacific War, never to return. In the 32nd year of Showa (1957), the heavy rain storm struck Isahaya, Nagasaki Prefecture, resulting in the deadly flash floods that swept through the city and destroyed a large number of houses. Many people lost their lives. So did my aunt and her three little children – my cousins. Luckily my father was away from home and escaped death. But he was left with no home, no family. My mother was one of the repatriates from Manchuria after the war. She and her family all came home alive except for the uncle who went to fight. But they lost their entire fortune. Shortly after, my father married my mother, and my brother and I were born.

Those who have lost their own houses or families, even their own lives, they are not just some other people who are unfortunate, whose tragedy we have little to do with. The similar tragedy can happen to any of us. What is worse still, it happens out of the blue. Besides disaster, many things can deprive us of our ordinary life. These are, for example, an accident, an illness, the death of a friend or family member, a trouble in personal relationships and unemployment. Any of them can happen to us any day. That is why we cannot stress the importance of our usual daily life too much. I never met those relatives of mine – uncles, aunt, and cousins, for they all passed away before I was born. However, what happened to them always stays in the back of my head and has a certain influence on my life. It teaches me the preciousness of our daily life. That is their legacy.

March, 2012 Yumiko Tanaka

田中由美子 プロフィール

1968	長崎県諫早市生まれ
1991	熊本女子大学卒業（現在の熊本県立大学）
1991-1999	東芝エンジニアリング株式会社勤務
1999	渡米（ニューヨーク）
2000-2005	ニューヨーク・比嘉良治ワークショップ受講
2004	ニューヨーク・栗田紘一郎ワークショップ受講
2006	帰国
2008-2009	TPOフォトスクール本科ゼミ第18期修了
2009-2012	株式会社冬青社勤務
2010-2012	普後均ワークショップ受講

www.yumikotanaka.com

Yumiko Tanaka Biography

Yumiko Tanaka was born and grew up in Nagasaki, Japan. She has been interested in art since her childhood. She graduated from Kumamoto Women's University in 1991. She moved to Tokyo and worked as a system engineer at Toshiba Engineering Corporation. Impressed by a friend's pictures, she bought a single-lens reflex camera in 1998.

In 1999 Yumiko moved to New York where she joined photography workshops of Yoshiharu Higa and Koichiro Kurita. She learned technical photography skills there for three years.

She came back to Japan in 2006. After finishing the 18th term of regular courses at TPO PHOTO SCHOOL, she started working at Gallery TOSEI & TOSEI publishing Co.,Ltd in 2009. She also joined the workshop of Hitoshi Fugo, where she started shooting her series of photographic work, entitled "The Precious Daily Life in Japan".

www.yumikotanaka.com

大切ないつもの暮らし

著者 田中由美子（たなかゆみこ）

2012年4月10日　第1刷印刷
2012年4月20日　第1刷発行

翻訳　　川田尚人
デザイン　石山さつき

発行者　髙橋国博
発行所　株式会社冬青社
　　　　〒164-0011 東京都中野区中央 5-18-20
　　　　Tel. 03-3380-7123　Fax. 03-3380-7121
　　　　振替　東京 3-135161
　　　　http://www.tosei-sha.jp/

印刷・製本　凸版印刷株式会社
Printing A.D.　杉山幸次
営業　　猪野直貴

The Precious Daily Life in Japan

Author/Photographer: Yumiko Tanaka

First Edition　: Apr. 10, 2012
First Published: Apr. 20, 2012

Translator: Hisato Kawata
Designer: Satsuki Ishiyama

Publisher: Kunihiro Takahashi
Published by TOSEI-SHA Publishing Co., Ltd
5-18-20 Chuo, Nakano-ku, Tokyo, Japan, 164-0011
Phone: +81-(0)3-3380-7123; Fax: +81-(0)3-3380-7121
Postal Account No: Tokyo 3-135161
http://www.tosei-sha.jp/

Printed & Bookbinding by TOPPAN PRINTING CO., LTD
Printing Art Director: Kouji Sugiyama
Business Manager: Naotaka Ino